100 Games
for One Player

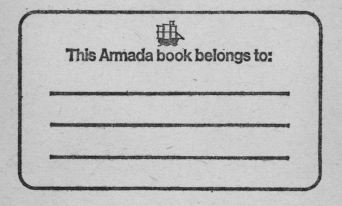

100 GAMES FOR ONE PLAYER

J. B. Pick

Illustrated by Anna Barnard

Armada

This collection of games has been
extracted from *180 Games for One Player*,
first published in 1954 by Phoenix House Ltd.
This edited and revised edition published by
Armada Books in 1974 and printed by
William Collins Sons & Co Ltd, Glasgow

CONTENTS

Two-Pack Patience

INTRODUCTION

This is a book of solo games, not puzzles or quizzes. What I call a puzzle is a set problem with one solution. There is no point in solving it again unless you have a bad memory, like me. But if you're like me you couldn't solve it in the first place. Each game of Patience, on the other hand, has as many solutions as there are favourable combinations of cards, and the cards never fall the same way twice. Solitaire, too, is not a problem so much as a game of problems. And it's the country of games that we're exploring.

Solo games, like all others, can be competitive. Long ago they used to play a game called 'Tit-tat-toe', marking the result to 'Old Nick' if neither player won. So you can always play against Old Nick.

Or in ball games you can play against a target score; against a record you have set; left hand can play right hand; one type of throw can play another. In this book that principle is applied with enthusiasm.

The organisation of the book is straightforward; under Outdoor Games will be found Ball Games, Eye Games (games of noticing, listing, searching), and Tool and Toy Games such as those played with a skipping rope. Under Indoor Games will be found Board and Table Games such as Solitaire, Patience Games, Pencil and Paper Games and games played silently in that most private of courts, the head.

As you play these you will invent other games of your own, and they will be the best.

J.B.P.

OUTDOOR GAMES

BALL GAMES

1. Bounce Ball

This is the simplest of 'record games' and will satisfy no one for longer than fifteen minutes at a stretch. Bounce a tennis ball on the ground and continue patting it down with the flat of your hand, counting the bounces to set up a record. After that, play to beat the record.

It is not so easy as it sounds: the height of the bounce begins to vary and the ball travels as though it were drunk and may become so disorderly you are forced to make an arrest. Which means – start again.

Still, when you begin to record scores in the hundreds it's time to think of other things. You can try patting with right and left hand alternately, and then turn to Two-ball Bounce Ball. In this game you do your best to pat down one tennis ball with the left hand, one with the right, counting the bounces of the right-hand ball. Frustrating.

2. Catch This Way

Throw up a tennis ball and catch it in both hands so often that you know you can never miss. Then try with the right hand only, then with the left. This is training. Now for the game.

Throw and catch in both hands, throw and catch in the right, throw and catch in the left; throw, twirl a half-turn so that you are facing the opposite way, catch in both hands; throw and twirl a half-turn and catch in the right; throw and twirl a half-turn and catch in the left; throw and twirl a full turn and catch in both hands; throw and twirl a full turn and catch in the right; throw and twirl a full turn and catch in the left. Now you have finished a 'set' and count 'one'. Continue smoothly on from the beginning until you have finished a second set, count 'two' and so on. Try to beat your own record. If you drop the ball, get out of order or forget who you are or what you're doing, begin again.

This dizzifier can be converted from a 'record' or 'counting of sets' game to a 'maze' or progressive game simply by increasing the number, variety and difficulty of catches, working out a long course which must be followed in order, without missing the ball, missing out a stage or forgetting whether you're in Ross-on-Wye or Kirkcudbright. For example:

Both hands; right hand; left hand; throw with the left and catch with the right; throw with the right and catch with the left; throw and clap before the double-hand catch; throw and clap before a right-hand catch; throw and clap before a left-hand catch; throw and clap twice before a double-hand catch; throw and clap twice before a right-hand catch; throw and clap twice before a left-hand catch; throw and clap three times through double, right and left; throw and clap at the back through double, right and left; half-twirl about between throw and catch through double, right and left; twirl about between throw and double-handed catch.

And if all this proves too short and too easy a course you can invent more difficult contortions to perform between throw and catch. When the rule is that you must catch the ball five times consecutively in each manner the game is called 'All Fives', which seems reasonable enough.

3. Drippy Steps

We invented this game once because we had a flight of five steps, a bed chair and a tennis ball. So that's what you need.

Place the bed chair at the top of the flight of steps, leaving space for the ball to bounce once when it drops off the chair. The front of the chair must be lowered, the back raised. You can adjust it to suit yourself.

Mark a line two feet from the bottom step. Stand behind the line and toss the ball on to the chair. Count the number of steps it bounces on.

The game is played with three goes to each turn (or if you prefer it, three turns to each go). If on your first throw the ball bounces on four steps, count four points; on the second five, count five; on the third three, count three. Your total score at that turn is twelve. The ball can bounce on each step as often as it likes, scoring only by step, not by number of bounces.

If the ball rolls off the side of the chair (which it does), off the side of the steps (which it does) or if it isn't caught cleanly after *one bounce* at the bottom, you don't score at that go.

Invent a cast of characters and play a tournament like golf. After everyone has had a turn, eliminate the bottom scores and carry on until there are only two contestants left and play a final.

The best way of distinguishing your characters is by style. We have a number of boring players who just hold the ball cupped in the hand and lob it gently into the air to plop down on to the chair like a bun on a cushion. Among these are Dump of the Netherlands and Billabong of Australia. Then there are players who spin it from right to left, like Biddler of the Faroe Islands, or who spin it from left to right like Lutanovic of the U.S.A.

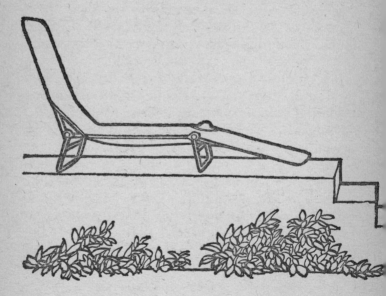

Or who flick from the back of the hand with fingers pointing towards the ground. This method is known as Standard Scandinavian Backspin and proves monotonously effective when employed by Thorwaldsen of Iceland, Boggis of Britain, Fjord of Norway, Krudsen of Sweden and a Stateless player named Tippicata.

You can invent all sorts of odd styles and players, who take a run up or toss it through their legs or throw two-handed or anything you like.

Drippy Steps

4. Left Against Right

Mark two parallel lines on the ground three feet apart and stand between them facing 'down the road'. Left hand bounces a tennis ball, right hand catches it and bounces back – a point is lost when a hand misses the ball, bounces it outside the court or behind the player or hits the player with the ball, or at any time when both hands are used. The game is played up to fifteen. The ball can be finger-spun, rolled, cut or bounced fast and direct; height, speed and direction should be varied continually, to surprise yourself; you may move your feet as much as you like and may be anywhere in Europe when you catch the ball, but you must be 'on the road' when you bounce it. In this game the right hand of a right-handed player has a greater initial advantage than in one-man fives or volley-ball, but practice helps.

5. One-man Fives

It's a mistake to imagine that the right hand of a right-handed player always defeats the left. He begins with the idea that his right hand is the more skilful so he works harder for the left, and it does wonders. Soon he grows irritated that this 'inferior' hand keeps winning and works harder for the right; but left has got the habit now and won't stop winning. Right gets rattled, recovers, concentrates and the real game begins. Every contest becomes a needle one and the player finishes as delighted at 'winning' or as disgruntled at 'losing' as if he had been playing a champion at Two-Fives instead of himself at One-Fives.

You only need a wall, an old tennis ball and a smooth patch of ground – tarmac, concrete, beaten-earth – to play this game. The court, ten feet by eight, with a service line three feet from and parallel to the wall, should be marked with paint, chalk or anything else you can think of. The simplest scoring system is: game played up to fifteen, service changing every five points, unless the score reaches fourteen-all, when a service changes after each point until one hand gains a lead of two. A simple system is necessary because the player must score in his head for 'both' hands; if he cheats or forgets, the game loses interest.

Right hand serves first from the service line, that is drops the ball and palm-hits it against the wall to bounce in court in left-hand's territory. Left hand takes service on the first bounce. Once the rally is under way the ball can be taken on first bounce or on the volley and hit against the wall to land anywhere in court. A point is lost when one hand hits out or on the second bounce, holds the ball or misses it.

Right hand hits continually to the right of the court; left hand immediately learns the backhand sweep and forces right to do the same. Right hand varies tactics and left hand counters. The mind and body play for the benefit of each hand equally, and have no difficulty in sliding from the effort to 'win for right' to the effort to 'win for left'. Played hard, the game is fast, skilful and surprising.

6. Roof Ball

You need a low, gently-sloping, gutterless roof, the eaves not more than five feet from the ground, and two tennis balls.

Roof Ball

Toss one ball on to the roof and, as it rolls down, throw the other. Catch the first and return it to the roof before the second drops. Repeat this as often as you can manage, counting as you catch each ball. Simple, of course . . .

At first you'll find yourself juggling angrily with both balls when you should be catching one, clutching at one while watching the other, jerking hopelessly hither when you ought to be thither – and all this before you've reached a count of twelve. The secret is: keep your eyes on the ball you are about to catch, acquire a rhythm and sweep both balls smoothly at an even height on to the roof.

When you begin to break one hundred regularly and can't be bothered to aim at huge targets, try three balls. This is fast and desperate work; if you break a hundred with three balls, let me know and I'll come and inspect your roof.

7. Target Ball

If you have available one wall and one pavement, draw a target on the wall with chalk and throw the ball at it to score points according to how near the bull's eye you get. After five goes, mark your score on the pavement with chalk and try to beat it.

Target Ball

EYE GAMES

8. Birds and Beasts

Almost too simple to be mentioned, this game is mentioned because the simplest and commonest things are often overlooked – sheep and sparrows and daisics, for instance.

On a walk in the country you can play off observation against observation: list in your mind the species of bird you see, the species of beast you see, and count them as you go. There's a rook, one bird; there's a cow, one beast; there's a dog, two beasts, and a rabbit three and a yellowhammer two. . . . It is cheating to *hear* a cuckoo and count it as a bird seen, you can argue with yourself whether to count a hen as bird or beast, and whether to cheat by counting a bull as one and a cow as two, but it is best to give Beasts the benefit of the doubt as you are unlikely to see as many varieties of animal as of bird.

Flowers can join in if you are level-headed, many-sided and able to count three lists at the same time; or flowers can play trees or you can hold a knock-out competitition, Birds against Beasts as far as Stumbly Stanton, Flowers against Trees from Stumbly Stanton to Nether Tripping, winner of One against winner of Two from Nether Tripping to Tickly Parva.

Birds and Beasts

You can vary the game if you are training to be a note-taker for the Ministry of Agriculture by counting ploughed fields against pasture, one crop against another, sheep against cows. You attain an intimate knowledge of your locality in this way, but everything within reason: if you count too many varieties of bird, beast and object you will end up counting pebbles, rusty tins, fence-posts, insects, outsects, grass-blades, buttercups and the windows in houses. The next step is counting the nurses in a mental home.

9. Listening

This comes under Eye Games because you use your ears. That's logic. We do so much seeing that we don't hear anything except the obvious.

Try when walking along simply to *listen*, and count the separate sounds you can hear. You will become bemused with surprise by the number of noises you have never noticed: birds, beasts, beetles, bees, buses, boots, boys and bulldozers; brays, bleats, boos, bawls, bangs, buzzes, booms and blurts; tweets, twitters, toots and trills; shushes and sighs; wails, whistles and whispers.

But don't try it on a main road or all you will hear are gears, grinds and growls.

The more you practise the more you will hear. Eventually it becomes a habit. Then try smells.

10. Names and Natures

Try to spot on shops, factories, warehouses, business name-plates, in telephone books, advertisements and newspapers, the most suitable names for members of each trade or profession. I have seen a Mr Death the butcher, Mr Law the solicitor and Mr Dent the garage man.

Or you can collect the names of firms which are simply peculiar – or in some cases downright impossible, such as the estate agents Button, Menhenett and Mutton. I know a Mr Pepper (a milkman, not a grocer), and a Mr Purple (a doorman, not a bishop). Don't ring up when you make a discovery and ask questions like 'Are you Smellie?' This would be uncouth.

11. Peculiar Things

It's easy to cheat at this game, so, if you catch yourself, disqualify yourself immediately. You win by collecting more Peculiar Things in May than in April, this week than last week or et cetera than so forth.

The Peculiar Things collected are sights seen as you trundle about. You don't see them if you look, but they are more peculiar if seen out of the corner of your eye, and if you look too vigorously for things that are peculiar you may miss things that are obvious and walk into a lamp-post.

The difficult part of the game is defining what is peculiar and how peculiar it is. Stretch the definition too far and you spoil the game. A bowler hat on a man is not common nowadays but is hardly peculiar. A bowler hat on a woman would be *very* peculiar. Twenty points for that, straight away. A steam roller is rare but not downright peculiar. Five points. A vintage car is only just a scoring object. Say, two points.

Here are a few scoring sights I've seen recently: a vase of flowers on the deck of a ship; a cat sitting in a butcher's window; a lady bathing with a flowered hat on; a railwayman chasing a balloon along the track.

Peculiar Things

12. Turn Left, Turn Right

This game could be as accurately titled 'Getting Lost', and parents may disapprove. It is best played in a town, only four times from the same starting-point and not too many times in the same neighbourhood or it becomes too easy.

Choose a place you know and can ask your way back to if you're stuck, begin walking, take the first turning to the left, first right, first left, first right and so on until you don't know where you are. Then get back to your starting-point without using the route by which you came. You will soon be an authority on the town in which you live and can give directions to taxi-drivers on how to get from the Town Hall to Round's Square and from High Street to Low Lane swimming-baths without going near the roundabout in Poltroons Road where there is always a whirlpool of cars, lorries, vans, bicycles and pedestrians with prams, shopping bags, briefcases, children, suitcases, ladders and suicidal tendencies.

The game can also be played in the country on a bike, maps forbidden.

TOOL AND
TOY GAMES

13. Battledore and Shuttlecock

There is no need to play battledore and shuttlecock with shuttlecock and battledore. You can play it just as well with badminton racket and shuttlecock, or tennis racket and tennis ball. Battledores, after all, are merely small and almost extinct bats or rackets.

The game consists in hitting ball or shuttlecock into the air and counting the number of times you can hit it up before missing, falling over or running into a wall. The secret is a steady, uniform and rhythmic pat. When you establish a record in the hundreds, the game has nothing more to offer you. Hitting a tennis ball hard against a wall with a tennis racket is much more exciting and much more useful; take the ball on the bounce or on the volley, and the more expert you get, the better you become at tennis.

14. Five Stones (Snobs)

This game is a technical marathon and can go on for ever. The variations given below are not the only ones, but should be enough. The game is often played as a contest but it probably arose, like many games, from one person playing idly with the material available – in this case, five pebbles. Learn an easy medium-height throw and watch the stones you're lifting.

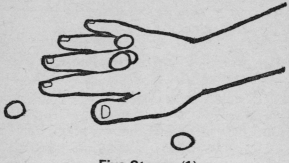

Five Stones (1)

(1) Throw up five pebbles and catch them first on the back, then in the palm of the hand. If one is caught, play continues; if not, start again. Stones on the ground are picked up in this way:

(2) Lay down all caught stones but one and throw this up; while it's airborne lift one of the dropped stones, catch the falling one and carry on throwing and lifting until all the stones are gathered.

(3) Lay the stones in a row, lift one and toss it up, before it falls pick another, with that in hand catch the first. Lay this aside, throw the one retained, pluck another and so on until they are all in hand.

(4) Lay the stones in a row, throw one, pick up two and catch the first as it falls. Repeat, plucking the remaining two.

(5) This time pick three and then one.
(6) Lift four at once.

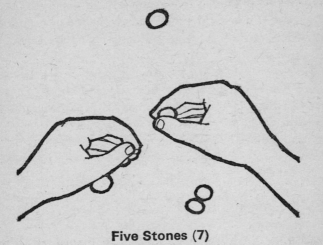

Five Stones (7)

(7) Make an eye with left thumb and forefinger, placing the side of the hand farthest from the eye to the ground. Throw one, lift one and pop it through the eye, catch the aerial stone and so on until all are popped.

(8) Take a stone in your palm and one between thumb and forefinger. Throw up the first and before catching it lay the second on the ground; throw up the one you've caught and lift the one on the ground. Repeat, increasing the number placed down by one each side until four are laid down and again picked up.

(9) Take four stones in hand, leaving one down, throw the four, lift the one and catch the airborne four. Increase

the number placed down and reduce the number thrown up until four are laid down and again picked up.

(10) Take four stones in hand and one between thumb and forefinger. Throw up the single stone, drop one of the four, catch the airborne one. Throw again, drop another and so on until all four have been dropped. Throw again and pluck all four.

(11) Lay the stones in a row, lift one and toss it up, before it falls pick another, that in hand catch the first. Go on throwing up all the stones you've gathered each time you pluck another.

If you make a mistake at any point, start again.

15. Hopscotch

Since in England this game is called Hopscotch because it came from Scotland, where it is called Peevers because the French word for stone is 'Pierre', it should probably be called Jumpfrench, but isn't.

It's a pavement game and a 'not-treading-on-the-line' game. There are a lot of hopscotch layouts but the commonest is the one illustrated here.

You play as follows: Flick a stone into bed 1. If it doesn't rest cleanly in the bed, with no part touching a line, start again. If it does, hop from the starting box to bed 2 in one hop; hop from 2 to 3; astride in 4 and 5, with a foot in each; into 6 on one foot; 7 and 8 with a foot in each; 9 on one foot. Go back the same way and jump out of the layout. Then flick the stone into bed 2, hop into 1, over 2 into 3 and so on as before.

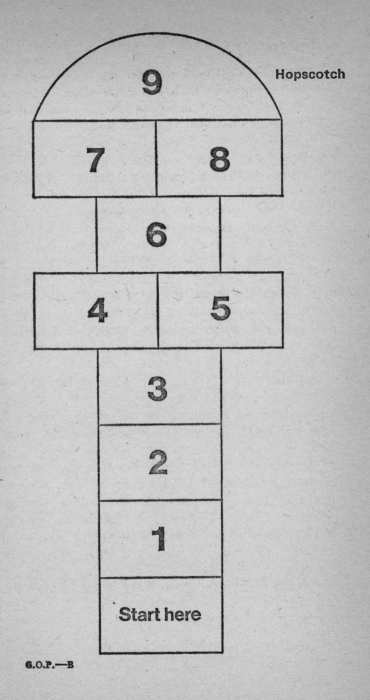

Hopscotch

Go through the maze until you have done all the beds without footling, toppling, stepping on a line, throwing or hopping in the wrong order, stopping or becoming recumbent.

A variation is to flick into 1, hop to it and tap the stone sidefooted into 2 and so on. Repeat, hopping on the other foot. Then do it with only one hop allowed from bed to bed.

Or do the whole thing with a ball bounced once and caught in each succeeding bed.

16. Marble Bowls

Four marbles of one colour can play bowls against four marbles of another, with a marble of a third colour as the 'jack'.

Call one 'rink' England and one Scotland, and roll a marble for each rink alternately, the aim of each rink being to place its marbles nearer the jack than those of the enemy. Most of the tactics of bowls itself can be used: blocking the path to the jack for your opponent, pushing an opponent's marble through and taking its place, breaking up the 'head' (or arrangement of marbles about the jack), picking off and driving away an opponent's marble and so on. The player must strive to build up a 'head' round the jack for each colour; he will soon be intensely concerned about which rink will win and astonished when he finds out.

It's just as good a game played with tennis balls or oranges.

17. Shell Race

At the seaside when the tide is ebbing, choose a runnel or a pool through which the current flows and find some shells – preferably shallow limpet shells. Call one Oxford and one Cambridge, mark a winning point, start them simultaneously and watch. When Oxford and Cambridge have fought it out through a series, use three, five, seven, ten boats and call the show Henley Regatta with each boat carefully selected and named. Or race one type of shell against another: big against small, deep against shallow, pale interiors against blue interiors, limpets against mussels. . . . Or play it with sticks in a stream.

18. Skimmers (Ducks and Drakes)

Flick a flat stone sideways to skip on the water. The stone must be fairly light and rounded and the throw low and even, made with a whip of the wrist.

See how many times you can make the stone skip before it sinks. Five or over is good. SPLASH is bad.

19. Skipping

A skip, if anyone doesn't know, consists of stepping with the left foot, hopping on the spot, stepping with the right foot, hopping on the spot and so on. Skipping with a rope means doing this while swinging a long rope, an end held in each hand, over the head and under the feet, the rope passing under the feet just when you hop.

A double-foot jump can also be used to clear the rope and it's possible to move forward by simply running, feet lifted high, over a travelling rope. The basic skip can be complicated by varying the speed of the rope, the height of the jump, by crossing the arms, reversing the swing and so on. A marathon game can easily be arranged in this way:

One double-foot jump to each turn for three forward turns of the rope.

One left-foot skip, one right-foot skip, one left-foot skip, one right-foot skip over forward turns of the rope.

Cross the arms and double-foot jump three times.

Uncross the arms and left-foot, right-foot, left-foot, right-foot.

Reverse the swing of the rope and double-foot jump three times.

Left-foot, right-foot, left-foot, right-foot.

Reverse the rope and double-foot jump.

Turn the rope forward twice to every double-foot jump. Double-foot jump three times.

If you make a mistake, hesitate, stumble, miss a stage, alter the order, giggle, scream, fall over or tie yourself hand and foot, you have lost. Every full course completed counts 'one'.

20. Standing Jump

The advantage of a contest like this is that you are sure to win.

Mark a chalk line and stand with both feet together, toes touching the line. Swing your arms and jump two-footed as far as you can.

Standing Jump

Mark where you get to and have another go. Make the mark at the heel of the foot nearest the starting line. Measure and record the distance of your longest jump and try to beat the record next time.

INDOOR GAMES

BOARD, TABLE AND FLOOR GAMES

21. Black and White

Using equal numbers of black-and-white counters on a forty-nine-cell board (seven rows of seven cells), place the blacks to fill three rows and three squares of the middle row, the whites to fill the other cells, leaving a single central square vacant.

The game is to move the blacks where whites were and whites where blacks were.

Blacks move from left to right or vertically down, by single-cell pushes or by jumping, as in draughts; whites move from right to left or vertically up in the same manner. Not only is there no compulsion to move counters alternately black and white, but the game cannot be solved if you do.

For instance, the pieces on the middle row can be exchanged in fifteen moves like this: move white, then successively two black, three white, three black, three white, two black, one white. This game is a sticky, long-drawn-out performance and I shouldn't start it late at night.

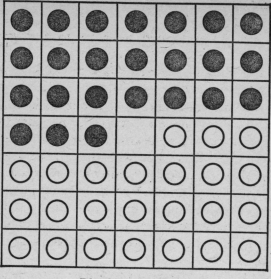

Black and White

22. Bottle Music

Arrange bottles or glasses in a row, graded according to the amount of water you have poured into each. In this way you will have organised a scale of notes which you can release by tapping the bottles.

Pour more water in or pour some out to adjust the notes, and with a bit of practice you will be able to play a tune recognisable enough to drive everyone out of the house.

23. Darts

To practise the game need not mean to play darts with yourself, but since to play darts with yourself does mean to practise the game – play darts with yourself. You can play 301 up in the usual way, hitting a 'double' to open your score, and finishing on a double to achieve the exact target total, throwing three darts for Jekyll, then three for Hyde; or, if you're ambidextrous, throw three darts with the right hand, then three with the left. (If you're not ambidextrous you soon will be after a week or two of that.)

Or you can play records. Pin a playing card on the dartboard and see how many times you can hit it with ten darts. Five times is tolerable, eight times good. Then throw to lodge six darts in one triangle – say, the 20 triangle.

Then play round the board: one dart in 1, one in 2, and so on. Only one throw at each compartment. If you hit, a point for you, if you miss, one against you. After that, p'ay for doubles. Every dart in a double compartment cou its five points to you, every failure one point against you. Play 100 up.

24. Eight Men

Arrange eight counters on a chessboard so that no two are on the same line in any direction, vertically, horizontally or diagonally.

25. Ground Ball

For this left- against right-hand game a small hard ball, rubber, plastic or cork, two tins or plastic mugs and a smooth carpeted, or uncarpeted floor are required. (The floor is a better playing area than the table because the ball travels a long way when missed.) Kneel down, holding one tin in each hand; place the left tin over the ball and sweep it away towards the right, lifting the tin clear. Right claps its tin down bang over the ball and sweeps it back to the left. First hand to miss a clean trap loses a point and the other hand serves to restart the game, which is played up to fifteen points.

26. Hare and Hounds

The game is played on a diagram drawn to the pattern shown. The object is for the hound counter to catch the hare counter before it can run from starting to finishing point, the two counters setting off from opposite corners of the diagram and moving alternately, hare first. To catch the hare means that the hound is in a position to move to the point on which the hare is standing when it is hound's turn to move. Both counters move one space at a time along connecting lines, but whereas the hare can move anywhere the hound cannot move along diagonals. Neither counter may move between the same two points more than three times in succession.

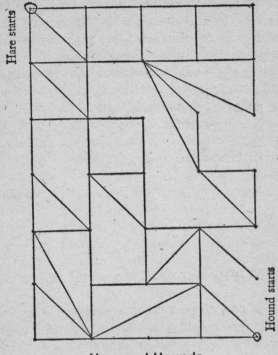

Hare and Hounds

27. One-man Ping-pong

You need a table-tennis ball, net, two bats, and a small table, say 4 ft by 3 ft., for this solo performance. The player stands at the net, a bat in each hand, and hits alternately left and right, over the net into the opposing court. Each

45

hand serves five points by dropping the ball on to the table on the service side and hitting it over the net so that it bounces on the receiving side. A hand loses a point if he hits into the net or off the table, misses, lets the ball bounce twice successively on one side of the net. An alternative method of play is to use one bat, hitting the ball with the front on one side of the net, with the back on the other. Poor practice for table-tennis proper, but a lively game of ping-pong improper.

28. Roll the Ace

Some people believe that you can exert an influence on rolling dice by willpower. Try it and see.

The game consists in shaking and rolling a single poker die, willing the ace to turn up. Mathematically, of course, the ace should appear in the proportion of one in six over a long series of throws. Just what is 'a long series of throws' I'm not competent to decide.

Simply rolling a die may seem a boring enough game and so it would be if you went on solidly hour after hour. But it can be done for five minutes, ten minutes or more at a stretch, rolling six times and recording the number of aces which turn up, rolling another batch of six, recording and so on. The business becomes fascinating when you begin to roll aces often enough to half-convince yourself that there may be something in this notion of 'mind influencing matter'. Break off when you grow tired because the more tired you grow, the fewer aces turn up, believe it or not. Change the die occasionally, roll from a cup and get someone else to record the score whenever possible.

29. Solitaire

Solitaire is normally played with marbles on a board with hollows arranged as in the diagram, but a court can, of course, be drawn, and counters used. One hole is left empty and a marble is moved by jumping over another in a vertical or horizontal line into a vacant space immediately beyond. The marble so overleapt is removed from the board. A ball can continue jumping as long as there are suitable 'backs' with a space beyond. Every move made *must* be a jump. The normal game begins with the centre hole vacant, the aim being to remove all the marbles from the board except one, which must finish in the centre hole. One solution is this: 19–17, 16–18 (29–17, 17–19), 30–18, 27–25 (22–24, 24–26), 31–23 (4–16, 16–28), 7–9, 10–8, 12–10, 3–11, 18–6 (1–3, 3–11), (13–27, 27–25), (21–7, 7–9), (33–31, 31–23), (10–8, 8–22, 22–24, 24–26, 26–12, 12–10), 5–17. Figures in brackets indicate the consecutive moves of a single marble.

Any hole may be chosen as the initial empty one.

Experience teaches that certain groups cannot be 'reduced'. Simply whipping off marbles whenever an opportunity presents itself is no way to solve the problems set by a solitaire board. The aim should always be to find a solution in the fewest possible moves.

You can make it more difficult by having some marbles which must not be shifted and can only be captured during the final move. An alternative is a single 'ball on the watch' which holds still until the end, when it takes the remaining balls and becomes last marble on the board.

			1	2	3		
			4	5	6		
7	8	9	10	11	12	13
14	15	16	17	18	19	20
21	22	23	24	25	26	27
			28	29	30		
			31	32	33		

Key to the Board

Solitaire

STRING GAMES

A six-foot length of string is formed into a loop by knotting the ends together. Patterns are made by winding the string about the hands and fingers. Some of the resulting figures are simple, some so complex as to require two players or a man with four hands. My choice has been made from those games I can manage myself, and is therefore severely limited. Kathleen Haddon's *Cat's Cradles from Many Lands* is the fullest source book. Most recorders use a special terminology invented by Doctors Rivers and Haddon, involving the terms 'radial', 'ulnar', 'palmar', 'dorsal', 'proximal', and 'distal'. I find this confusing. My only definition is: by the 'nearer' of two or more strings I mean the one nearer the body of the player.

30. Cat's Cradle

This figure is often known as 'Opening One', because it is the basic figure with which many other patterns begin. Take the string on the hands so that it runs behind the little finger and thumb of each hand and across the palm. With the back of the right index finger take the left palm string from below and return. With the back of the left index finger take the right palm string from below and return.

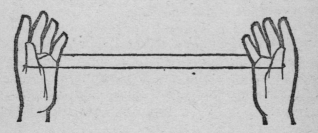

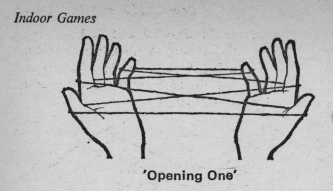

'Opening One'

31. Bed

'Opening One'. Put the thumbs over index loops, and into little finger loops from below; take the nearer strings of the little finger loops with the backs of the thumbs to return over index loops. Put the little fingers under index loops and with their backs 'hook' the nearer index strings and return under the other index strings. You have made your bed – now try and lie in it.

32. Eskimo House

'Opening One'. Turn your palms towards you, close the fingers of both hands over all strings except the one nearest you, throw this string over the backs of your hands and return them to the normal position, palms facing one another. You now have a new string which passes across the backs of the hands, runs straight between the hands on the little finger side and forms a cross on the thumb side.

Pass the thumbs over this near 'back of the hand' string and below all the other strings. With the backs of the thumbs 'hook' the farther 'back of the hand' string and return. Slip the loops off the backs of the hands over the fingers on to the palm and extend.

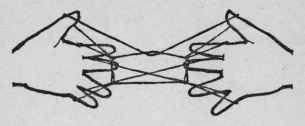

Eskimo House

33. Fly

Hook one end of the loop over the left thumb, pass the double string across the back of the hand, insert the right thumb into the other end of the loop and pull tight, making sure that the two strings of the loop are not crossed.

Insert the right little finger between the back of the left hand and the double string from below and return.

Insert the left little finger between the right little finger loop and the right thumb loop against the right palm, hook both right thumb strings towards you and return.

Lift the strings crossing the back of the left hand over all five fingers, and separate the hands.

By quickly half-turning both hands the fly can be made to move. Slap the hands together, release the little fingers and the fly is gone.

34. Lightning

Lay the string loop on the table in the form of a figure eight, one oval towards you, the other away from you.

Insert index fingers into the far oval, thumbs into the near oval, draw the hands apart sideways, then turn them upwards away from you into their normal position, with palms towards one another, and the strings of the loops on both thumbs and index fingers crossing one another.

Insert the thumbs into the index finger loops from below, lift the nearer index string and return.

Pass each middle finger towards you over one string, with its back lift the next and return.

Pass the ring fingers towards you over one string, lift the next and return.

Pass little fingers towards you over one string, with their backs lift the next and return.

Pass the thumbs over the other strings to rest on the nearer string of the little finger loops near the little fingers.

Release the thumb loops and throw them over the other strings.

Press down sharply with the thumbs and the lightning will flash into sight. Perhaps.

35. Moon

'Opening One'. Take the farthest string in the mouth and return over other strings, releasing little finger loops without pulling the figure tight.

Transfer thumb loops to little fingers by inserting little fingers from above, hooking the near thumb string and returning. Insert index fingers into the mouth loop from below and extend, letting go with the mouth. There are now two strings on the index fingers. Lift the lower string over and off the index fingers and draw the figure out.

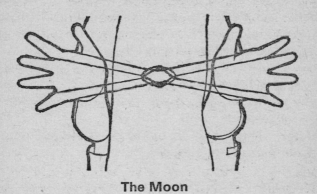

The Moon

36. Moon Gone Dark

Make the moon figure and lay it on the table. Place the left thumb and index finger into the former index loops from above, and the right thumb and index finger into the former little finger loops from above. Pass thumbs and index fingers down, bring them up again through the centre of the figure and extend. Insert thumbs and index fingers into the centre of the figure and extend once more.

TIDDLEY-WINK GAMES

37. Counter Battle

This game was invented as a contest between two players, but a single player can enjoy it, Yorkshire against Lancashire, Shropshire against the Isle of Wight, Architects against Sanitary Inspectors, Vikings against Picto-Scots, Angles against Curves, Alfred against the Cakes. . . . Arrange ten or twelve counters of one colour in line at one end of a blanketed table, ten or twelve of another colour at the other end, both lines the same distance from a new-penny-sized chalk circle in the centre. The aim is to sweep the enemy from the field.

If one counter lands on another so as to overlap it, the counter underneath is dead and removed forthwith from the board.

If a counter touches an enemy counter but fails to overlap it, that counter may move again but not to continue the attack, only to escape the inevitable counter's counter-attack.

If a counter overlaps an enemy it may move again to attack another and so on as long as it remains successful.

If a counter lodges cleanly in the centre circle all enemy counters already within a hand-span of the circle become prisoners, and are moved to one side, but enemy counters entering the danger area afterwards do not.

If an enemy lands in the circle on top of the first counter, the prisoners are freed and all counters of the first colour within a hand-span of the circle become prisoners in their turn.

If it lands in the circle to touch the occupying power without overlapping, it may escape, but if it lands inside without touching, it too becomes a prisoner.

If a counter is flicked off the table it becomes a casualty.

When all the counters of one colour are prisoners or dead, the game is over, and if the two sides fight again the winning side starts with as many more counters than its opponents as were left on the field at the end of the game.

The contest usually begins with a rush for the centre circle, then an assault on this circle by the enemy. The first to occupy the circle should win.

38. Free for All

Empty out on to the field of play all the tiddleywinks you can find and then begin flicking them furiously into the pot. Time yourself from the moment you tiddle the first wink to the moment when the last wink is tiddled. Then try to beat your record.

The more winks the better. But always start with the same number or you might accuse yourself of cheating, and quarrel.

39. Tiddley-wink Football

For this game a thin blanket must be spread over the surface of a table and at each end an egg-cup placed for goal. Five tiddley-winks of one colour are arranged opposite five tiddley-winks of another colour in teams of three forwards, one half and one back, with a tiddley-wink of a third colour in the centre to serve as 'ball'.

55

As captain of the Reds, 'flick off' the ball where you wish. As captain of the Greens, flick a man to land so that he touches the ball. If he succeeds in touching the ball you can flick the ball direct and if you can land it on another Green player you can flick the ball again; as soon as you are near enough the enemy egg-cup, shoot for goal. If Green fails to touch the ball, Red plays to touch it and so on alternately. A man is offside if no opponent stands between him and the goal. It is a foul to land a man on top of an opponent and a free flick is awarded against the offender. Ten minutes each way.

Select each team with care, name and mark each player, watch him and 'drop' him with a thud if he fails his side. Every team quickly develops a style and 'form' of its own, some teams remain as consistent as Leeds United, others skelter from the heights to the depths like Chelsea. Players reveal marked individuality on the field and you find out surprising things about historical personages by selecting them to play in a game of tiddley-wink football. That Oscar Wilde should be so talented as spearhead of the Irish attack seems odd – especially when you note how ineffective George Bernard Shaw is on the left wing. Nelson, certainly; Burns, yes; but Gladstone . . . ! *His* prowess at full-back comes as a shock. It might interest readers to know, and even if it doesn't it's my duty to record the fact, that an Elizabethan team with Marlowe and Shakespeare in the forward line, proved almost un-beatable in the English League, and that a team repre-senting British Literature beat Scandinavia 3—0, Russia 1—0, Germany 3—2, France 2—0, drew with Italy 1—1, lost to Spain 1—2 and to Greece 1—2.

But there is no need to stick to literature. Musicians,

soldiers and seamen are all able to field strong teams; the British Painters' five is surprisingly lively; the Scientists are full of ideas and the Politicians most untrustworthy, with only Canning and Gladstone showing real talent for the game. What this proves I hesitate to say.

40. Toy Soldiers

H. G. Wells in his book *Little Wars* worked on a scheme of play with toy soldiers which could be followed by one player or by two.

His approach was unrealistic. For example, in his game, if equal numbers of soldiers of both sides came in contact the contest was in effect 'drawn'. But in fact small numbers have often defeated and destroyed large numbers. Superior fire-power or better individual marksmanship or higher morale might decide the issue. And if it comes to hand-to-hand fighting, as in this old-fashioned warfare it often does, a big good 'un is better than a small ditto.

Again, in H. G. Wells's game, control of a position is decided simply by the number of troops of either side present at the spot: the larger body of troops forces the smaller to retreat. But in reality a small body of troops might stupidly refuse to retreat and succeed in holding a position against odds. Altogether there is too little room in the Wells game for chance and individuality.

In laying out a game of toy soldiers, it is essential that a battle should have some purpose and that it should be fought out on definite and convincing terrain. Two mobs propelled into mass conflict on a bare floor may satisfy a love of slaughter but don't make for an interesting game.

Indoor Games

Toy soldiers should be played outside on a weed-grown terrace with every weed a strategic position, or on a patch of flat ground scattered with stones, every stone a vantage point, or it can be played indoors with hills formed by blocks of wood, buildings of cardboard and so on. One side should be defending and the other attacking a prepared position.

The defending side should be arranged to cover all approaches with the greatest available firepower, remembering that a machine-gunner is worth three riflemen, and that well-armed regulars are a more formidable force than such common irregulars as cowboys, Red Indians and naked savages. Artillery should be placed where it can be used to the greatest advantage and has the widest possible field of fire. The question of an ambush, of a line of retreat, of first and second lines of defence, of bodies of reserve troops and so on must all be considered.

As for the attacking force – the line of advance, the most suitable strength for different groups, the best cover, the most economical and effective use of armoured vehicles and cavalry will all have to be thought out.

In this game sides move alternately, as many men as the general wishes in whatever direction he wishes but no infantry man more than three inches at a time, no cavalryman more than four and no armoured vehicle more than six. No man may 'fly' over the heads of enemies or of his own troops. When he meets opposition he must fight or retreat.

At each turn a side may fire off all its armament once at any available target. A number of graded missiles must be collected for this purpose: for artillery, marbles; for machine-guns and groups of four riflemen, a very small pebble. If during the course of action a group is reduced from four to three the size of the missile must also be reduced.

If the group sinks to two men, they must either join up with another group, and cannot fire on that move, or they must retreat or wait in readiness for hand-to-hand fighting. Irregulars armed with lances, spears, tomahawks, cricket bats, carters' whips, hunting-horns, lariats, boxing-gloves, pikes, halberds, swords, cutlasses or bowie knives cannot fire at all, and that's that. Milkmaids with buckets had better retire. Irregulars can only fight at close quarters.

Firing consists simply in tossing (not throwing) the missile towards the enemy. A man is killed when he's knocked over and for convenience the bodies are removed from the field of battle by the miraculous arrival of vast aerial fingers. If a man falls so that he is leaning against a comrade like a drunkard coming out of a pub he is merely wounded and can begin to walk to the rear, where he can recover and return to the fray after three moves. An armoured vehicle is only put out of action when hit by an artillery shell. A cannon is put out of action when hit by an enemy artillery shell or when the gun crew is killed.

Obviously the defending side has the advantage, for infantry cannot fire while being moved. Attackers should always be supported, therefore, by covering fire, shielded by armoured vehicles, which *can* fire, and must get to close quarters as soon as possible.

The rules for hand-to-hand fighting are these. If opponents face one another as individuals each in turn is held by the head (headless men are not allowed on the field of battle) and swung firmly but not violently against the enemy so that his stand catches him below the knee. The first to fall is dead, poor fellow. If neither falls, the combatants must separate.

When one man is kneeling he is at a disadvantage which, literally, is his funeral.

A cavalry man is unseated if an infantry man gets close enough to 'tap' his horse and a spare foot soldier takes his place.

When there is a melée and men from both sides are mixed together a missile is suspended over the mob and dropped like a bomb. The casualties are then removed. No aeroplanes are allowed because retaliation against them is impossible to arrange.

There are no rules regarding the time when a group or an army must retreat. You as the general make all decisions, remembering that you must save enough men from a defeated force to form the nucleus of an army which can fight again another day. If at the end of a battle the defeated side has less than ten men left alive, the war is over.

Every battle should be fought bearing in mind who won the last battle – the defeated army, for instance, defending its capital city. Five successive victories must be considered to finish a campaign – less if you, as general, decide that defeats have been overwhelming.

After Blues have been defeated once or twice you can always alter command, of course, and put in charge a man with different ideas. This increases interest and makes for realism. Besides, the younger generation must be given its chance.

PENCIL AND PAPER GAMES

41. Cut-out Poems

Snip out a lot of separate words from newspapers, magazines, brochures about holidays in Nicaragua and leaflets advertising free rubbish, but not from the book Dad took out of the Library last Tuesday.

Make sure that there is a supply of useful nouns and ordinary verbs.

Then put them on a tray and shift them about until they begin to make a queer sort of sense. Once they begin to make a queer sort of sense you may find you can build a queer sort of poem out of them.

You are allowed to use the odd 'and' or 'to' or 'but' or 'with' or 'for' or 'from' even if it isn't among the cut-out words – but no nouns or verbs or adjectives.

Start with a big collection of words or it is too difficult. Here are some examples which I did:

> *'Iron justice gives service,' said the King.*
> *When things are perfect, people take to crime.*
>   *

Safe in their bank of moss
Under the foreign moon.
*

Smoothly poised where folded people are,
The bright steel moon.

42. Forecasts

Association football, I have heard, is a popular game for twenty-two players; filling in pool coupons is a more popular game for several million players, but the second game is played 'solo'. In other words you have all played 'forecasts' at one time or another, by betting on a horse-race, failing to spot the lady, or telling Arthur Spragg there will be rain before evening; and if you view the forecasting *itself* as the important thing, betting on the result becomes unnecessary. Not that I'm viewing this as a moral question, but no one can afford to bet on everything, and anyone who insists on trying is a bore with his 5p on which rain-drop will travel the pane pane first, which hen will cluck first, which duck will quack first and which quack duck first. You can only guess about raindrops on window panes, and there's neither skill nor sense in blind guessing.

Before any reasonable forecast can be tried, information of all kinds must be gathered. For instance, if you want to predict the England cricket team to play Australia, the form of players in past seasons, in previous Tests, in the games before the match itself, particularly the form of those who met the Australians, must be carefully re-corded. The names, characters, prejudices and preferences of the selectors must be considered. And here we come to the most important point.

The game of forecasts consists in attempting to prophesy the team which *will* be selected, not in deciding the team which in your opinion *should* be selected. These names may or may not be the same.

When the officially chosen players become known, award yourself a point for every one picked both by you and by the selectors, even though you think Suchandsuch useless because he can't field and are certain that Soandso, who is a valuable change-bowler, should play in his place.

Keep a record of your score throughout the season and consider yourself good if you get fifty per cent right in a year when the English team is losing.

And of course there is plenty to do when there are no cricket teams to be selected: consider records, form, jockeys, course, condition and forecast the result of a horse-race. Consider team records and those of individual players on particular grounds, occasions and against particular opponents, together with weather conditions and et ceteras before forecasting the result of a football match. (It is practically impossible to forecast the exact score, unless by means of extra-sensory perception: Arsenal, Tottenham or draw is the most which can be expected.)

There's an alarming amount of work to be done: stocks and shares, election results, budgets, hockey matches, marriages, crop failures, motor-races, weather changes, best-sellers, fashions in clothes and hats and books and names, government policy, theatrical successes, theatrical flops, French Prime Ministers, industrial output. . . . It would be as well to study sociology, palmistry, psychology, astrology, parapsychology, statistics, economics, meteorology, mathematics, anthropology, ostropology, gnomology, apólogy and cynics. (Also, if possible, cybernetics.)

Once you begin playing Forecasts seriously you will view the addicts of such trivial pastimes as solving crossword puzzles and investigating the structure of the atom with good-natured contempt. Crossword puzzlers may need *Rogets Thesaurus, The Oxford Dictionary,* an encyclopedia or two, books of synonyms and quotations, the *Dictionary of National Biography* and a history of literature, but you will need a library with everything in it from the *Economist* to the *Beano,* as well as the powers of a magician, the sharpness of a barrister, the industry of a scholar and the patience of Job.

43. Line Maze

Mark three rows of six dots, the dots about half an inch apart; the object is to draw lines from every dot to every other dot without touching with the pencil point any dot but your objective, and without touching any line already drawn. You will start with jolly optimism and end raving.

44. Origins

Go through a page of a book or a column of a newspaper, write down the first word of more than three letters you meet beginning with 'a', then with 'b' and so on through the alphabet as far as you like. Your job is to guess the language of derivation and original meaning of each word, with a dictionary as referee – the decision resting on the derivation rather than the definition. Mark a point to yourself for each success, a point against you for every failure. Where no proper derivation is given you neither lose nor gain a point. Old Nick gains one – so watch it.

45. Parody

The principle is simple – an example of a near-rhyme which leads me to think of the line as the possible opening to a poem by – well, let's see. ... The principle, then, is: set yourself a subject and compose a poem in the manner of any poet you like – or, preferably, dislike. Certain poets are sitting targets – Wordsworth as to daffodils, William Blake as innocent, Ogden Nash with outrageous puns. But many with a distinctive style are more difficult, and those without one are almost impossible. In any case, why shoot a dead bird? And why romp only in fields of poetry? There are lots of prose opportunities: write a report on a Royal Occasion in the style of the *Daily Express*, or a murder trial from the *News of the World*, or a description of a journey in a train by Richmal Crompton, John Buchan, Eric Ambler or Enid Blyton.

46. Radio

This game consists in recognising – voices, pieces of music, singers, authors and so forth on the radio, without consulting the *Radio Times* and before the announcer can tell you who's who and what's what. The best way to do this is to look up the programme in the newspaper, which as a rule simply says 'Concert', 'Sports Desk' or something of the sort, wait until one has been running a short while and switch on. If a piece of music is being played, guess the composer and the work or the singer and the song. If you can't do that, guess when it was composed.

When the piece ends, switch off until you calculate the next has begun and at the end of the programme check

Parody

your suggestions against the list of items in the *Radio Times*. Music lovers will hate you, but that's not my business.

If the programme is one of the familiar chat affairs like Any Questions, Twenty Questions, Petticoat Line or Silly Answers, guessing the voices should be as easy as eating ice-cream, and a party political pep-talk should not be difficult, but the business may be ticklish if it is a discussion between experts on the Relation of the Cost of Living Index to the Cost of Dying Outdex.

67

Record the number of items or speakers in each programme and your correct guesses, then compare your results for the 'season' – say a week or a month or three months – with the maximum possible score. But don't bore your friends by telling them how well you've done.

47. Transformation

Set yourself the task of moving on paper from one word to another by altering one letter at a time. For instance, from HEAD to FOOT: HEAD, HEED, HOED, HOOD, FOOD, FOOT. The aim is to make the journey using the fewest possible linking words. I'm sure that this game, though it is usually played as a competitition between two or more players, started as a solo one. Medieval monks probably played it in Latin in their heads at night.

HEAD GAMES

48. List against List

Another counting game? Well, there is a distinction between counting games and listing games. You cannot
count features of a passing landscape when lying in bed
with your eyes closed trying to get to sleep, but you can
make lists, and making lists is a good way of getting to
sleep. This doesn't mean it is boring. You cannot sleep
when you are bored – in other words you cannot sleep
when your mind is empty except for the notion that you
wish you were asleep. Nor can you sleep when you are
worried or concentrating hard on a serious subject.

Making a single list is too easy and requires too little
concentration. Trying to hold two competing lists in your
head, on the contrary, sends you off in no time. It helps
when you forget whether or not you have already counted
Brahms in your list of German composers and have to
start again. The whole business becomes blissfully confusing and before you know where you are it is morning.

You even find yourself looking forward to discovering
next night just how many German composers you *can*
remember, for you know you had reached twenty when
you fell asleep grumbling about Brahms. And was Meyer-
beer German? And are Austrians counted?

The question whether German composers will defeat French painters becomes of some importance. It must not become too important or you will do detailed daytime research, which is cheating, concentrate too energetically and lie awake all night. For making lists may become a habit. It is even possible to imagine you have achieved something important by listing *all* British wild flowers, film comedians, famous fat men, Worcestershire cricketers, mad poets, Foreign Ministers, Italian cars, Napoleon's marshals, Football League teams, members of the United Nations, or States in the U.S.A. Many scholars suffer from this delusion.

However, to return to the game. It is a mistake to match German composers with, say, German philosophers. The names will form a Teutonic glue from which you will be unable to free yourself. Be bold. A surprising contest can be staged between French poets and Australian cricketers. And how about chocolate manufacturers against biscuit manufacturers, or books you've read versus pop groups? There is a maze of possibilities into which only the brave will stray.

49. Stepping-Stones

This game consists in passing from one word to another by association of ideas through three 'categories' – for instance from 'harp' to 'party' through 'comedians', 'politics' and 'horse-racing'.

Nine phrases may be used as stepping-stones and although the player must pass through each category to reach his goal he need not divide his stepping-stones into three for each category, he need not use the name of a category as one of his stepping-stones nor need he use all nine stones if he doesn't want to. Here is a four-bound passage from 'harp' to 'party' through 'comedians', 'politics' and 'horse-racing'.

HARP. Harpo Marx. Karl Marx. (We are now in politics.) Winston Churchill. (Who owned racehorses.) Conservatives. PARTY. You must not use *more* than nine stepping-stones.

In performing this dance in the theatre of your head it is essential to set yourself words and categories at random – without thinking, the words 'bottle' and 'turnip', the categories 'Music', 'the sea' and 'Religion'. If you choose your words and categories too deliberately you are kicking-off before the whistle has blown, or, to put it more plainly, cheating. To prove that the task need not be difficult I'll try the problem set above without thinking too hard.

BOTTLE. Cork. Mute. Trombone. (We are now in music.) Sea-Shanties. (We are now, obviously, in the sea.) The sky. Heaven. (We are now, I claim, in religion.) Rain. Crop. TURNIP.

Of course, it is much easier to solve the problem on paper than in the head; for this reason the use of paper is against the rules. Count your failures against your successes, and give up the game when it becomes too simple, or try ever more difficult ways of threading between THIS and THAT.

50. Taboo

The game consists in attempting to keep in your 'mind's

eye' a selected image (say a circle, a square or a cross) for as long as possible without dreaming, relating it to other images or in any way letting your attention wander. It is easy to *think* that your attention is fixed but as soon as you think 'my attention is fixed', it is not, or you would be unable to think about your attention. In other words this task is very difficult. There is no need to stop when you have mastered it. You can decide on a long series of thoughts, images or objects to follow in sequence, any other thoughts, images or objects being taboo. You win if you manage this sequence without losing your way, getting out of order or allowing your mind to drift. This is a severe, tiring test. Cheating is easy but pointless.

51. Teams

This is a 'soporific' game. Imagine you are selecting a football team of composers to play a football team of generals. Each player in a football team has a different function, each composer a different function, each composer a different style and intention. Your aim is to choose the right man for each job; you select a composer not on the basis of any knowledge you may have of his life character, health, physique and ability as a footballer but entirely on the evidence of his work. You select a general on the evidence of his career.

The centre-forward should be a dashing, hard-working, powerful player – Beethoven would certainly be impressive in the position. Never mind the fact that he was wrathful and deaf, it's his music that matters. And centre-half, now. . . . Obviously there is a world of difference between

Mozart and Tchaikovsky – just as there is a world of difference between the positions of centre-back and outside-left.

As for the generals – Montrose is a dasher, Napoleon an opportunist, Eisenhower an organiser. . . . Then there are painters, poets, novelists, politicians, lots of possibilities. And if you cannot resist trying out some of these teams, there is always tiddley-wink football.

PATIENCE GAMES

INTRODUCTION

There must be well over five hundred Patience games; they have never been collected in a single volume and I doubt if they ever will be. Certainly you have not the patience to play them.

Whether those included here are 'the best' I cannot say without playing every known game repeatedly, a life's work in itself, but they are interesting. Many 'Patiences' differ little from their fellows except in the fanciful nature of their layout, and I have been careful to choose games for their merit as games, not for their merit as tableaux.

Below is a glossary of terms commonly used in describing the game of Patience. I'm sorry it is not possible to describe Patience games without all these terms, but it is simplest that way, once you have learnt them.

Block. A block occurs whenever you can't go on playing, according to the rules, with the cards available.

Column. A vertical 'file' of cards, 'down' the table 'from North to South'. In 'close column' the cards overlap, in 'open column' they are spaced apart.

Depot. Depots are those layout positions from which exposed cards may be played to foundations and on which other exposed cards may often be packed. Depots are packed in this way to open up the game and expose cards which may later be played to foundations.

Discard pile. A pile formed by cards which when dealt from the pack will not play to foundations or depots. Often known as the 'rubbish heap' or 'waste heap'.

Exposed cards. Uncovered cards playable to foundations or depots, generally those at the bottom of a column, the end of a row, the top of a pile or turned up from the pack.

Foundation. A base card (not necessarily an ace) on which other cards are built in sequence: the foundation row is the decisive row in all games which require foundations.

Grace. The privilege of an exceptional move when a block occurs.

Reserve. A number of cards dealt aside and only used under circumstances which vary according to the particular game.

Row. Cards laid horizontally across the table, usually from left to right.

Sequence. Cards following one another in correct order. An ascending sequence runs from low to high, a descending sequence from high to low.

A complete ascending sequence on, for example, six, would be: seven, eight, nine, ten, jack, queen, king, ace, two, three, four, five. (And vice versa for descending, of course.)

Where this seems necessary my descriptions state whether cards are to be dealt 'face up' or 'face down'; where no specification is made cards are dealt face upwards.

Finally, a note: Patience can only be played with a well-shuffled pack.

ONE-PACK PATIENCE

52. Agnes

Deal from left to right a row of seven cards face upward and just below that a row of six, then of five, and so on until you have laid out a triangle of twenty-eight cards, with a bottom row of a single card as its apex; you now have seven depot columns of varying length. The next card turned up from the pack starts the foundation row; the three fellow foundation cards (i.e. of the same denomination) join the first as they become exposed in play.

The object of the game is to build thirteen cards on each foundation in ascending sequence of suit.

The card for the time being at the bottom of each depot column is exposed, and may be played to foundations in upward sequence of suit and to depots in downward sequence red on red, black on black, *regardless of suit*.

Sequences and parts of sequences ending in an exposed card may be moved in block from depot to depot if they will fit.

As soon as all suitable cards from the first deal have been played, seven more cards are dealt, one to the foot of each column, and so on until the pack has been dealt through. All seven cards must be dealt each time before any may be moved.

When all the cards of a column have been played you may fill the resulting space with any exposed card or sequence of cards *of the same suit*.

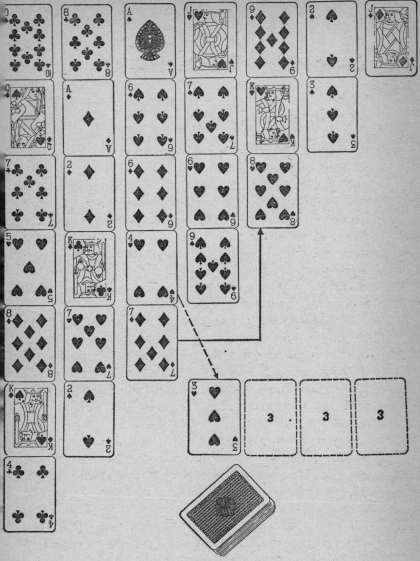

Agnes

Bisley

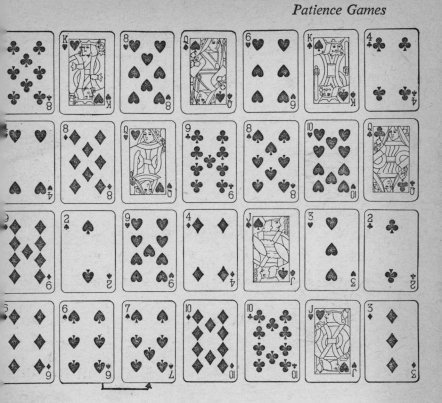

Bisley

53. Bisley

Deal the whole pack from left to right into four rows of thirteen cards each, to form thirteen depot columns of four cards each, the four aces being placed at the top of the pack and dealt into the first four places on the top row to form foundations.

Kings are laid aside to form other foundations as they become available.

The bottom card of each depot column is exposed and playable to ace foundations in upward sequence of suit, to king foundations in downward sequence of suit, to king foundations in downward sequence of suit, and to other depots in upward *and* downward sequence of suit, the order being reversible at will.

Sequences and parts of sequences may *not* be played from one depot to another.

When all the cards of a depot column have been played the resulting space is filled by a single exposed depot card.

When a king and an ace sequence 'meet', the king sequence is built on to the ace, the final object of the game being to build the entire pack in sequence of suit on aces.

54. Burleigh

Deal from left to right two rows of six cards each.

Aces are placed to form foundations as they appear in play, and the object of the game is to build the pack from aces to kings in ascending sequence of suit.

The twelve original lay-out cards must be arranged to form ascending or descending sequences of suit by moving one card which will fit on top of another.

When all possible cards have been moved, play the top card of the pack to foundations or depots if it will fit. If it will not fit, lay it aside and take the card from the *bottom* of the pack; continue playing to foundations or depots from the bottom of the pack until either you are blocked or the temporarily laid-aside card will fit somewhere. Then deal from the top of the pack once more.

A sequence or part of a sequence ending in an exposed card may be moved in block from one depot to another if it will fit.

55. Castle

Deal the pack into thirteen depot piles: first a row of five cards face downward; above it a row of four; above this a row of three; above this a single card. Two more sets of cards are dealt face down in the same order on top of the first. Then a final set of thirteen cards is dealt *face upward* in the same order on top of the lay-out. Exposed cards are the top card for the time being of each depot pile.

When one is played the card beneath is turned face up, becomes available and may be played to foundation aces in ascending sequence of suit or to depots in descending sequence of alternate colour.

A sequence or part of a sequence ending in an exposed card may be played in block from depot to depot if it will fit.

When all the cards of a depot pile have been played the resulting space may be filled with an exposed card or sequence from a depot.

Aces are laid aside to form foundations as they become available in play, the object of the game being to build the whole pack on foundations. No redeal is allowed.

56. Cousins Twice Removed

Deal the pack from left to right one card at a time to form a row. When two cards separated by two others are alike in suit or rank, play the left one on to the right and close up the row. The object is to form the whole pack into three piles by the time the last card is dealt. Utterly skill-less.

57. Demon

It isn't as bad as its name; the patience rarely goes through, but play is perfectly straightforward.

Deal thirteen cards face up to form a stock pile, then a row of four cards face up, each card to head a depot column, lastly a single card face up to begin a foundation row. The other three cards of the same denomination join the first foundation as they appear in play.

The object of the game is to build thirteen cards on each foundation in ascending sequence of suit, ace played on king, two on ace.

The bottom card for the time being of each depot column, the top card for the time being of stock are exposed and playable to foundations in upward sequence of suit, to depots in descending sequence of alternate colour. A sequence or part of a sequence ending in an exposed card may be moved in block from one depot to another if it will fit.

When all the cards of a depot column have been played the resulting space must at once be filled by the top card of stock until stock is exhausted, when the space may be filled or not, as you like, with any exposed card.

Deal from the pack three cards at a time. The top card of the packet may be played to foundations or depots if it will fit. If it *is* played the second card of the packet becomes available, and if that's played, the third is exposed. The pack is continually lifted and redealt three cards at a time until only two cards are left. These are dealt separately and may be played.

One 'grace' is allowed: if you are blocked you may move one top card from a foundation packet to the top or bottom of a depot column if it will fit.

58. Fan

Deal face upward seventeen depot 'fans' of three cards each, and one depot of a single card. The single depot card and the right-hand card for the time being of each depot fan is exposed and playable to foundations in ascending and to depots in descending sequence of suit. No sequence or part of a sequence may be moved in block from depot to depot.

When all the cards of a depot have been played the resulting space may be filled only by an exposed king.

The Fan

Exposed aces and aces exposed in play are moved to form
a foundation row, the object of the game being to build the
pack on foundations.

It is fatal to play a card to a depot containing a low card
of the same suit. Nor should, say, a jack be played to a
queen of clubs when the ace of clubs is imprisoned in the
depot like Bert Laggs in a queue for Cup Final tickets;
the only hope of freeing the ace is to fill a space with the
king of clubs, and transfer the queen to it. This cannot be
done if the queen is covered by the jack.

59. Follow On

Deal from left to right a row of six depot cards. As aces appear in play lay them aside to form foundations. The object is to build the pack on foundations in ascending sequence and in correct order of suits, the rotation being hearts, clubs, diamonds, spades – that is, a heart can only be laid on a spade, a club on a heart, a diamond on a club and a spade on a diamond.

The top card for the time being of each depot pile and the top card for the time being of the rubbish-heap are exposed and playable to foundations in ascending sequence and correct rotation, to depots in descending sequence and correct rotation.

Cards are dealt from the pack one at a time to foundations or depots if they will fit, if not, to the rubbish-heap, which may be turned once and redealt.

60. Fours

This game is played with a pack from which twos, threes, fours, fives and sixes have been removed. Deal a row of four cards face upward. If there are two of the same denomination exposed move one from right to left on top of the other.

Deal across another four cards on top of the first four or, if any have been moved, into the spaces they occupied. Again, move any matching card from right to left on top of its twin, deal again and so on dumpedido. No card must be moved until the row is complete.

Whenever four cards of the same value, irrespective of suit, are collected together, lay the quartet aside and continue as before. When a matching card is shifted on to its twin and reveals another of the same value beneath, this card is also moved from right to left to join the family.

The pack is continually lifted and redealt until all the cards are laid aside in groups of four, in which case you've won, or until the same cards recur in the same order again and again, in which case you've lost.

For each redeal the packets must be lifted face upwards in the correct order – first the second packet from the left is placed on the packet at the extreme left, then the packet third from the left is laid on top and lastly the right-hand packet. Turn the pack face down and deal again from the top.

61. King Albert

This is a good game but tends to become clogged and sticky unless you are an experienced patience player with a wide selection of cards up a wide sleeve.

A triangle of forty-five cards is dealt face upward in rows from the top row of nine cards to the bottom row of one. The object of the game is to build the pack on foundations in ascending sequence of alternate colour, aces being moved to form foundations as they are exposed in play. Exposed cards are the bottom card for the time being of each column and all stock cards. These may be played *singly* to foundations or to depots in descending sequence of alternate colour.

When all the cards of a depot column have been played, the resulting space may be filled by any single exposed card, but it is not always advisable to fill the gap; the existence of spaces will prove invaluable later. When there is *one* space in a layout you are entitled to move a sequence of *two* cards from one column to another provided it fits, when there are *two* spaces you may move a sequence of *four* or less, three spaces eight or less, four spaces sixteen or less. You may at any time play cards back from foundations to depots provided they fit. Only one deal is allowed.

62. Labyrinth

For this game a telescopic arm is of more use than an acute brain. You lay out four aces in the distance, by lurching across the table. The object of the game is to build the pack on these foundation cards in ascending sequence of suit.

Deal face upwards from left to right a row of eight cards immediately below the aces. Any suitable cards in this row are played to foundations, and the spaces created filled by dealing into them from left to right. After this, deal another row of eight immediately below the first and play to foundations, but do not fill spaces: the first row is the only one reinforced after battle. Then deal another row, play to foundations and so on until the pack is exhausted. A complete row must be dealt out before cards in it are played.

When the layout has been established a new phase of the game begins. The top and the bottom rows of the maze are taken as being exposed and any card may be played to foundations if it will fit. When a card is played from the top row it is held to expose the card immediately below, and so on; when a card is played from the bottom row it exposes the card immediately above, and when *that* is played – et cetera. If the patience is blocked, one suitable card may be played from any row to a foundation in the hope that this will set the game moving. If it doesn't you've lost.

63. Martha

Lay aside the aces to form a foundation row and deal the rest of the pack into twelve depot piles of four cards each.

The top card for the time being of each depot packet is exposed and playable to foundations in ascending sequence of suit, to depots in descending sequence and alternate colour. Sequences and parts of sequences ending in an exposed card may be moved in block from one depot to another if they will fit, but when all the cards of a pile have been played the resulting space may only be filled by a single exposed card. This is a very easy game.

64. Puss in Corner

The four aces form a foundation square. Deal from stock a card at a time to any one of four discard piles. The top card of each discard pile is exposed; after each set of four cards has been dealt, play available exposed cards to foundations in ascending sequence of colour. One redeal is allowed, the discard packets being lifted from right to left.

65. Pyramid

A skill-less patience for the impatient. Deal a pyramid of twenty-eight cards in seven rows, one card at the top, a row of seven at the bottom. The two second-row cards overlap left and right lower corners of the top card, and so on.

All cards in the bottom row are exposed and available to begin with; when two adjacent cards are played they uncover one in the row above, which becomes available in its turn. The dealing card and the top card for the time being of the discard pile are also available for 'pairing'.

The object of the game is to lay aside the whole pack in pairs of cards whose pips add up to 13, jack counting 11, queen 12 and kings being laid aside singly.

66. Raglan

This patience is unusual in that the whole pack is loosed in full cry upon the table before play begins.

First lay four aces face upward as foundations, then deal six stock cards face up to a safe position away from the teeth of the pack. Deal across from left to right a row of nine cards face upward, followed by rows of 8, 7, 6, 5, 4 and 3 immediately below one another, to form nine depot columns, the three columns on the left consisting of seven cards, the next six, the next five, the next four, the next three, the next two and the column on the extreme right one. Eh? Well, try it and see. The object is to build the pack in ascending sequence of suit on foundations.

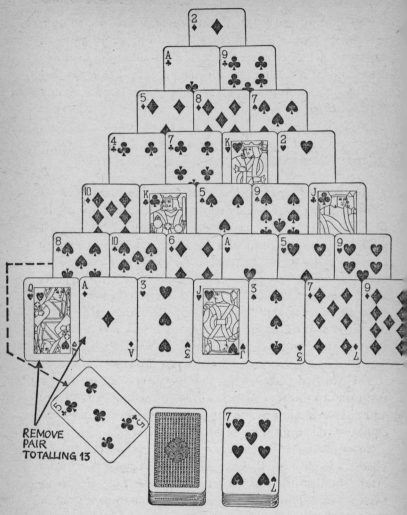

REMOVE
PAIR
TOTALLING 13

Pyramid

The bottom card for the time being of each depot column and the six stock cards are exposed and playable *singly* to depots in descending sequence of alternate colour and to foundations in ascending sequence of suit. The space left when a depot column is played out may be filled with any exposed card.

67. Royal Family

Take the four kings from a pack, lay them face upward to form an index row, and shuffle the remaining republic of cards. Deal face upwards in three rows twelve depot packets of four cards each. If any queens, jacks, or tens are exposed at the top of a packet, the queens are placed on the right and a little lower than their husbands, the jacks in a similar position on the left and the tens directly below, drawing to them the other cards of their suits in descending sequence, till each ten is topped by an ace and each king is surrounded by his family of subjects. In other words, tens are the foundation cards, the rest ornaments.

The exposed cards on the depot packets can be moved from one to another if they will fit in ascending sequence and alternate colour. The object is to free first nines, then eights, sevens and so on to build on the tens.

Spaces created when a depot packet is exhausted are not filled until play is blocked; the centre depot row is then lifted, shuffled and dealt out again. There must always be twelve packets but in the second deal they may consist of three, two or even single cards.

68. Sevens

Deal from left to right a row of seven cards, the first six face down, the last one face up; below this a row of six, five face down, the last face up; a row of five, four face down and the last face up, and so on, the bottom row consisting of one face-up card. The bottom card for the time being of each depot column is exposed and playable to foundation aces – which are laid aside as they appear in play – in ascending sequence of suit, to depots in descending sequence of alternate colour. Face-down cards are turned face up when exposed.

When all the cards of a depot have been played the resulting space may only be filled by an exposed king, who should be ashamed of himself. Turn from the pack three cards at a time, playing the top card of each packet to foundations or depots if it will fit; if so the next card can be played and so on. If not, turn up another packet of three. The top card of the discard pile is always available.

The pack may be turned and redealt in sets of three until you are finally blocked. When only two cards are left to turn up they are examined and played separately.

69. Six by Six

Deal from left to right face upward six rows of six cards each to form, surprisingly enough, six depot columns. Then deal from the pack one card at a time to depots or foundations if it will fit, if not to the left-hand column, which is a discard depot. Aces are laid aside to form foundations as they appear.

The bottom card for the time being of each column is exposed and playable to foundations in ascending sequence of suit or to depots in descending sequence regardless of suit.

A confusing complication is that a sequence or part of a sequence *in suit* ending in an exposed card, may be played at any time from one depot to another, so long as the highest card is in descending sequence regardless of suit to the bottom card of the column to which it is played.

When all the cards of a depot column have been played, the resulting space may be filled by the next card dealt from the pack or by any exposed card. Only one deal is allowed.

70. Stonewall

These stone walls are too high. Only Joshua, trumpet and all, is likely to force this patience through.

Deal from left to right six rows of six cards each to form six depot columns, the first, third and fifth rows face down, the others face up. Then lay out the remaining sixteen cards flat on their backs to form a reserve.

The bottom card for the time being of each depot column and all the cards of reserve are exposed and playable to foundation aces (which are laid aside as they appear in play) in ascending sequence of suit, and to depots in descending sequence of colour. When a face-down card is freed it is turned face up and becomes available.

Sequences and parts of sequences ending in an exposed card may be played from depot to depot if they will fit.

When all the cards of a depot column have been played the resulting space may be filled by any exposed card or sequence.

71. Thirteens

Deal out the pack in four rows of thirteen cards, each row overlapping the one above, to form thirteen depot columns of four cards. Move each king to the top of his column, aces to a foundation row as they become available. The card for the time being at the bottom of each column is exposed and playable to foundations in upward sequence of suit and to depots in downward sequence regardless of suit.

The object of the game is to build the whole pack on the four foundation aces.

Sequences or parts of sequences ending in an exposed card may be moved in block from depot to depot. When all the cards of a column have been played the resulting space is *not* filled.

72. Travellers

Deal the cards face upwards into three rows of four, then deal on to these rows until the whole pack is laid out stone cold in three rows of four packets, four cards in each packet. The four cards left over you immediately hire as travellers and place them in a packet of their own.

The aim is to pack all denominations together in order, starting with a packet of four aces at the left of the top row, then a packet of four twos, then a packet of four threes, finishing with four queens at the right of the bottom row. For the duration of this game all kings are dethroned and prove as useless as most ex-kings.

The method is to take the top 'traveller' and place him at the bottom of his rightful packet – if he's a five, he goes to the left-hand packet of the second row, if he's a ten to the second packet from the left on the bottom row and so on. And, of course, so forth.

The top lodger of the packet to which the rolling stone has returned mossless gives up his bed and rolls off home himself, selfishly pushing out another fellow; this cox-and-box process continues until an ex-king hiding in one of the boarding-houses turns up at the top of a packet, or until a packet is completed. In both cases a second card from the travellers' packet begins his journey, the king being deported to a rubbish-heap. If a king turns up in the travellers' packet he's discarded and the next card is used. This game urgently requires the exercise of no skill whatever.

TWO-PACK PATIENCE

73. Above and Below

For this game two packs are kept separate.

Deal one card, face upward, as an index. The foundations are formed by four cards (one of each suit) next in sequence *above* the index card, and four cards (one of each suit) next in sequence *below* the index card. As they appear in play, the higher cards are placed on the left, the lower on the right of the index. (Cards of the same denomination as the index card are laid on it as they appear in play.) Suppose the index card to be a five, the sixes are built on in ascending sequence of suit, the fours in descending sequence of suit.

Deal from the pack, one card at a time, to foundations if possible; if not, deal from left to right across a row of four discard piles; the top card for the time being of each discard pile is exposed and playable to foundations. Cards may also be played from one foundation packet to another if they will fit.

When both packs have been dealt through, lift the discard piles from left to right, turn face down and deal from the top of the pack without shuffling.

If by the time this pack has been dealt through all the cards are not built on foundations, each foundation crowned with its second index card from the index pile, you have lost.

Above and Below

74. Carlton

Shuffle two packs together and deal from left to right a row of eight cards face upwards; then a row of seven overlapping the top row; then six and so on down to one, to form a layout of eight depot columns.

The bottom card for the time being is exposed and playable to foundation aces – which are laid aside to form a foundation row as they appear in play – in ascending sequence of suit, and to depots in descending sequence of alternate colour, the object of the game being to build both packs on foundations. A sequence or part of a sequence ending in an exposed card may be played from depot to depot if it will fit.

When all the cards of a column have been played, the resulting space must be filled with any exposed card or sequence.

When all available cards have been played, deal from left to right one card face upwards to the bottom of each depot column, overlapping the card already there. No card may be played at this turn until every depot has received its addition.

Continue to play and deal in this way until the pack is exhausted. Only one deal through is allowed.

75. Colorado

Deal from left to right two rows of ten cards each to form twenty depot-discard piles. Lay aside as they become available one ace and one king of each suit to form foundations.

Deal from the pack, one card at a time, to foundations in ascending sequence of suit, or if a card will not fit, to any depot pile you choose, regardless of suit or sequence. The top card for the time being of each depot pile is exposed and playable to foundations, but may *not* be moved to any other depot pile.

When all the cards of a depot have been played, the resulting space is filled from stock.

76. Constitution

To play this game is like wading through glue. Remove kings and queens from the pack, lay aside aces as foundations, and reassure them – they won't be troubled. Deal four rows of eight cards each and prepare for the worst.

The object of the game is to build on foundation aces in ascending sequence of suit to jacks.

The top card for the time being of each *top row* depot packet is available for play to foundations; from no other row may cards be played directly to foundations. Top cards of top row packets may also be played to other top row piles in descending sequence of alternate colour if they will fit, and all cards in the second row are available for play to top row packets.

When a space occurs in the top row it is filled by the second-row card just below it; when a space occurs in the second row it is immediately filled from the bottom row and a space in the bottom row is filled from the pack. Cards from the pack and the bottom rows get into play only in this manner.

77. Deuces

Place the eight deuces (twos) in two rows to form foundations, which must be built in ascending sequence of suit up to aces. Deal round them on three sides, four above and three on each side, ten depot cards.

Deal from the pack one card at a time to foundations in ascending, to depots in descending, sequence of suit; or, if a card will not fit, to a discard pile, the top card of which is always available. The top card for the time being of each depot pile is also exposed and playable to foundations or to other depots. A sequence or part of a sequence may be moved in block from one depot to another if it will fit.

When all the cards of a depot have been played the resulting space may be filled from the discard pile or from stock; it may *not* be filled by another depot card.

78. Display

Place a single card at the top left of the board and deal from the pack one card at a time to the 'display' layout or to any one of three discard piles, the top card for the time being of each discard pile being always available.

Whatever is the value of the initial card, a card of the denomination immediately below it in sequence must be laid to its right, and a card of the denomination immediately above it in sequence must be laid directly below it. Supposing the first card to be an eight, a seven must be laid to its right, a six next to that and so on until a descending sequence of thirteen cards regardless of suit forms a row from left to right across the board. Below the

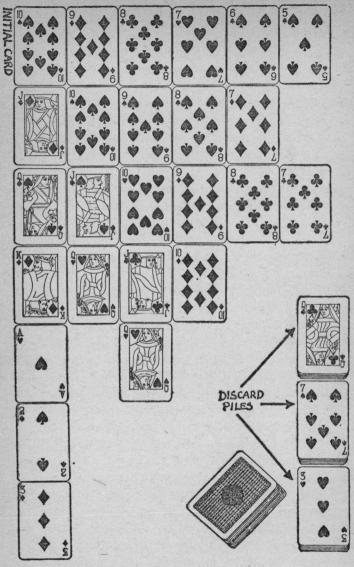

Display

eight a nine must be laid, below the nine a ten and so on until eight cards form a column in ascending sequence down the board. Below the seven an eight must be laid, below the six a seven and so on until either the whole pack is displayed on the board in eight rows of thirteen cards each in descending sequence and in thirteen columns of eight cards each in ascending sequence, or you find yourself blocked owing to a mistake made in packing on the discard piles.

Lay out the top row as soon as you can and try as far as possible to keep the columns running abreast.

79. Eights

Deal from left to right eight rows of eight cards, each row overlapping the row above, so that the layout consists of eight depot columns. The bottom card for the time being of each column is exposed and playable to foundations in ascending sequence of suit or to depots in descending sequence regardless of suit.

The object is to build on aces, which are placed to form foundations as exposed in play.

A sequence or part of a sequence *in suit* may be played at any time from depot to depot, provided it fits, irrespective of suit, with the card on which it is played. A sequence not in suit cannot be played in this way.

When all the cards of a column have been played the resulting space may be filled by an exposed card or a sequence in suit.

When all available cards have been played cards are dealt one at a time from the top of the pack to foundations or depots if they will fit; if not, to the left-hand depot column.

Only one deal through the pack is allowed.

80. Falling Star

Deal from left to right eleven cards face upwards. These are the 'stars' which must fall in due order on to foundations – starting with the star on the extreme right of the row and working across to the left.

The next card turned from the pack denotes foundations and is laid by the Mayor of your town to begin a foundation row immediately beneath the row of stars. As other cards of the same denomination appear in play they take their places in the foundation row. Now deal a depot row of eight cards.

The object is to build all the cards on foundations in ascending sequence of alternate colour until each foundation is crowned by a card of the denomination immediately below the original foundation card in sequence.

The stars remain unmoved in the heavens until the right-hand one can be packed on a foundation. The bottom card for the time being of each depot column, the dealing card and the top card for the time being of the discard pile are exposed and playable to foundations in ascending sequence of alternate colour. A sequence or part of a sequence ending in an exposed card may be played in block from one depot to another but *not* from a depot to a space.

When all suitable cards have been played deal from the pack one card at a time to foundations, depots or, if a card will not fit, to a discard pile, the top card of which is always available. If all the cards of a depot have been played the resulting space is filled by a card from the pack or the discard pile.

81. General's Patience

Not, like many a general's patience, short.

Deal from left to right a reserve row of thirteen cards, then turn up the next three from the pack. Choose one for the first foundation and with the remaining two begin a depot row of nine cards, dealing out the other seven at once. As the matching foundation cards appear place them with the first. The top card for the time being of each depot pile is exposed and playable to foundations in ascending sequence of suit, to depots in descending sequence of alternate colour. Sequences and parts of sequences ending in an exposed card may be moved in block from one depot to another.

When all the cards of a depot have been played the resulting space may be filled by any exposed card or sequence. The right-hand card for the time being of the reserve row is also available for play to foundations *only*.

Deal from the pack one card at a time to foundations, depots or, if a card will not fit, to a discard pile, the top card of which is always available.

If in the original reserve row all the suits are blocked – that is, a higher card is on the right of a lower in each suit – you may deal a fresh thirteen. You are also allowed to transpose any two cards in the row.

82. Heads and Tails

Deal out a depot row of eight cards, below this a reserve row consisting of eight packets of eleven cards each, below this again a second depot row of eight cards.

As they appear in play lay aside as foundations one ace and one king of each suit, the aces to be built upon in ascending, the kings in descending, sequence of suit. The top card for the time being of each depot pile is exposed and playable to foundations as described and to depots in sequence of suit up or down – the direction reversed at will.

Cards from the reserve packets of the middle row can only be obtained when all the cards of a depot pile have been played. The resulting space is then filled by the top card of the reserve packet immediately above or below it.

If the whole of a reserve packet has been played, the space may be filled by the top card of the reserve packet immediately to its left, or if the extreme left-hand packet is exhausted, by the top card of the reserve packet on the extreme right.

83. Intelligence

Deal from left to right face upwards eighteen depot fans of three cards, laying aside aces to form foundations as they appear, and replacing them from stock. The right-hand card for the time being of each fan is exposed and playable to foundations in ascending sequence of suit, to depots in ascending or descending sequence of suit, the order reversed at will. Sequences and parts of sequences cannot be moved in block from depot to depot.

When all the cards of a fan have been played, they are replaced from the pack – this is the only way in which stock cards can enter the game, and the only way in which spaces may be filled.

Two redeals are allowed. Lift all the fans, shuffle the pack and lay out again.

84. Intruders

Place eight aces to form foundations, then deal a depot column of four cards. Deal across to reserve a row of eight cards and play all available cards from reserve to foundations in ascending sequence of suit and to depots in descending sequence of suit. Then deal across another row of eight cards, overlapping the first, and play to foundations and depots.

The bottom card of each reserve column formed in this way and the top card of each depot pile are exposed and playable to depots or foundations. Sequences and parts of sequences ending in an exposed card may be moved in block from one depot to another if they will fit, but no card may be played from one reserve column to another.

When all the cards of a depot have been played the resulting space is filled from reserve or from the pack.

Continue to deal across to reserve and play until only four cards are left in the pack. These are 'intruders' and form another depot column. From now on no card may be played from reserve to the first depot column, but only to intruders or foundations. Intruders may be played to depots, depots to intruders and both to foundations.

The object is to build the whole pack on aces in suit up to kings.

85. K.C.

Deal face upward twelve depot packets of four cards each.
Aces are laid aside to form foundations as they appear in
play. The top card of each depot packet is exposed and
playable to foundations in ascending, and to depots in
descending, sequence of suit. Sequences and parts of
sequences ending in an exposed card may be moved in
block from one depot to another. When a packet is exhausted the resulting space may be filled by any single
exposed card.

Deal from the pack one card at a time to foundations
and depots, or if a card will not fit, to a discard pile, the
top card for the time being of which is always available.

86. King Columns

Deal the whole pack from left to right across four depot
rows of three cards each, counting as you do so, one, two,
three, four, and so on up to queen. Whenever the card
dealt corresponds with the call, place the card aside to a
reserve packet, and replace it from the pack. Whenever a
king appears, lay it aside to help form two foundation
rows, four kings of different suits in a vertical column on
the right of the layout, four on the left. The object of the
game is to build the pack in descending sequence of suit on
left-hand kings, in ascending sequence of suit on right-hand
kings.

The top card for the time being of each depot packet is
exposed and playable to foundations but *not* to other
depots. If there is a choice (say, between two exposed nines

107

of clubs) you may look at the card below each available one before making a decision.

When play is blocked turn up the top card of the reserve packet and take in hand the depot packet which it indicates – for example, if you turn up a three, lift the third depot packet, that is, the right-hand packet of the top row; if you turn up a five, lift the middle packet on the second row, and so on. All the cards in hand are available and may be played to foundations.

When no more can be played from hand, arrange the remaining hand-cards in the order you think most useful and replace the packet where it came from. If two foundation packets are built to a point at which they meet in sequence, cards from one may be transferred to the other if this will help the game forward. No redeal is allowed. Rather an odd patience.

87. Lady's Patience

Deal face upwards four depot rows of four cards each, leave a central space for foundations, and deal another four depot rows.

The object of the game is to build in ascending sequence of suit on foundation aces, which are therefore moved into the central space as exposed in play.

The left-hand card for the time being of each left depot and the right-hand card for the time being of each right depot row is exposed and playable singly to foundations in ascending sequence of suit, and singly to depots in descending sequence regardless of suit.

When all available cards of the layout have been played, deal from the top of the pack one card at a time to foundations and depots or, if a card will not fit, to a discard pile, the top card of which is always exposed and playable. When a depot row is exhausted the space may only be filled by a single king. A single card, a sequence or part of a sequence may at any time be played *back from foundations* to depots if it will fit, regardless of suit. This is the only manner in which sequences can be moved in block. They may *not* be played from depot to depot.

Only one deal through the pack is allowed.

88. Miss Milligan

Deal from left to right a depot row of eight cards face upwards. Lay aside any aces to form a foundation row, to be joined by other aces as they are exposed in play.

The object of the game is to build on foundations in ascending sequence of suit.

When all available cards in the first row have been played, eight more are dealt across, one to each column or space. Only when all eight have been dealt may any exposed card be played. The bottom card for the time being of each depot column is exposed and playable to foundations in ascending sequence of suit and to depots in descending sequence of alternate colour. A complete sequence ending in an exposed card may be moved in block from one depot to another if it will fit, but part of such a sequence may not.

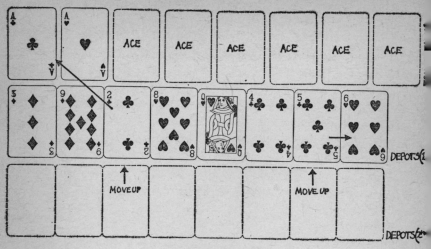

Miss Milligan

Play continues until the pack has been dealt through and either the patience is blocked or all cards are built on ace packets in sequence of suit up to king.

When the patience is blocked you are allowed to perform an operation known as 'waiving'. Lift the bottom card of any column and play the card or sequence immediately beneath it, if it will fit, before playing the 'waived' card itself. This 'waived' card must be playable. You can continue to waive cards like mad so long as you waive them one at a time.

110

89. Napoleon's Square

If you did not know that Napoleon was square, now is your chance to learn.

Deal twelve depot piles of four cards along three sides of a rectangle; move aces to the centre as foundations when they appear in play.

The object is to build the whole pack on aces in ascending sequence of suit up to kings.

The top card for the time being of each depot pile is exposed and playable to foundations in ascending and to depots in descending sequence of suit. Sequences and parts of sequences ending in an exposed card may be moved in block from one depot to another, if they will fit.

When all the cards of a depot pile have been played, the resulting space is filled by any exposed card or sequence.

Play by dealing one card at a time from the pack to foundations, depots or, if a card will not fit, to a discard pile, the top card of which is always available.

90. Odds and Evens

Deal four rows of four cards each, leave a space, then deal another four rows of four cards each. As they turn up in the deal or during play, move to the centre space one ace and one deuce of each suit to form foundations.

The object of the game is to build the whole pack on aces by twos in sequence of suit 3, 5, 7, 9, etc., through king up to queen; on deuces 4, 6, 8, etc., through queen up to king.

Choose which block of sixteen is to be 'active' and which 'passive'. All the cards of the active block are exposed and playable to foundations, but only the bottom card for the time being of each column on the passive side. If cards of the same value are available in both blocks the passive one must be taken. The vacancy caused when an active card is moved, is at once filled from the pack or the discard pile, but when a passive card is played it exposes the one above it in column, which becomes exposed and playable in its turn.

When a column is exhausted, the resulting space is filled from the pack or the discard pile.

Deal from the pack one card at a time to foundations or a discard pile, the top card of which is always available.

Deal through the pack and, when you are blocked, turn the discard pile and lay out six grace cards. If any of these is playable, continue the game.

91. Red and Black

Place the eight aces to form a foundation row. Then deal from left to right face upward a depot row of eight cards.

The object of the game is to build the whole pack in ascending sequence of suit on aces.

The bottom card for the time being of each depot column, the dealing card and the top card for the time being of the discard pile are exposed and playable singly to foundations in ascending sequence of suit and singly to depots in descending sequence of alternate colour. No sequence or part of a sequence may be moved in block.

When all the cards of a depot column have been played the resulting space must be filled by dealing into it from the pack, or if all the cards have been dealt, by the top card from the discard pile. The space must *not* be filled by a depot card.

When all available cards in the original layout have been played, deal one card at a time from the pack to foundations and depots, or if a card will not fit, to a discard pile. When the pack has been dealt through, turn the discard pile and re-deal. This may be done once only.

92. Reform

Deal, from left to right, a row of eleven cards face upwards. One ace and one king of each suit are taken as dealt to form foundations and their places filled from the pack. Any cards which will fit are played to foundation aces in ascending sequence and to foundation kings in descending sequence of suit, and their places filled from the pack before a second row of cards is dealt across, overlapping the first. Their replacements may also be played, replaced and so on. When each row after the first has been dealt the card for the time being at the bottom of the left-hand column and the card for the time being at the bottom of each of the two right-hand columns are exposed and playable.

When the whole pack has been dealt through, the bottom card for the time being of every depot column is exposed and playable to foundation aces in ascending sequence of suit, to foundation kings in descending sequence of suit, and to depots in upward *and* downward sequence of suit, an upward sequence changed to a downward and vice versa at any time. When a card has been played it exposes the one beneath, which may also be played, and so on. Only single cards may be moved, not sequences in block.

When all available cards have been played, lift the left-hand depot column, lay it on the next one and so on across the row, then turn the pack face down and deal as before. No third deal is allowed. One grace in each suit is permissible at any time during each deal through the pack; that is, a single card may be moved from one depot to another if it will fit.

93. Reserves

Deal in three rows four deuces, one from each suit, and eight aces as foundations.

The object of the game is to build on the top row of aces (one from each suit) in ascending sequence of suit to kings; on the second row of aces in suit by twos to kings; on the deuces in suit by twos to queens.

Deal two depot rows of eight cards each. These cards are all available for play to foundations but not to one another. When one has been played the resulting space is filled from the discard pile or if that is empty, from the pack.

Deal from the pack one card at a time to foundations or if a card will not fit to a discard pile, the top card of which is always available.

94. Round Dozen

Deal round three circles of twelve cards, face upwards, each overlapping the one previously dealt, to form twelve depots of three cards each.

The object of the game is to build the whole pack in ascending sequence of suit on foundation aces to kings, and on foundation kings in descending sequence of suit to aces.

Exposed aces and kings and those exposed in play are laid aside to form foundations, until the foundations consist of one ace and one king of each suit. The outer card for the time being of each depot, the dealing card and the top card for the time being of the discard pile are exposed and playable to foundations as described or to depots singly in upward and downward sequence of suit, upward changing to downward and vice versa whenever possible and convenient. No sequence or part of a sequence may be played in block from depot to depot.

When all available cards have been played from the original lay-out, deal from the pack one card at a time to foundations and depots, or if a card will not fit, to a discard pile, the top card of which is always available.

When all the cards of a depot have been played the resulting space may be filled with any single exposed card.

95. Star

Discard all kings but a single king of hearts; place him in the centre of the board surrounded by the eight aces in the form of a star.

The object of the game, astoundingly enough, is to build the whole pack on aces in ascending sequence of suit.

Deal round from the pack one card outside each ace. If a two appears, play it to the proper foundation and deal into its place from the pack. When all suitable cards have been played to foundations, deal round again, play to foundations whenever possible, fill vacancies and deal a third time. The outer card for the time being of each 'point' of the star is now considered to be exposed and playable in ascending sequence of suit to foundations and in descending sequence of suit to depots. A sequence or part of a sequence ending in an exposed card may be moved in block from one depot to another if it will fit.

Deal from the pack one card at a time to foundations and depots or, if a card will not fit, to a discard pile, the top card of which is always exposed and playable.

When all the cards of a depot have been played, the resulting space may be filled by any exposed card or sequence ending in an exposed card.

96. Streatham Common

Deal four rows of ten cards face upwards, each row overlapping the one above, to form ten depot columns.

The object of the game is to build the pack in ascending

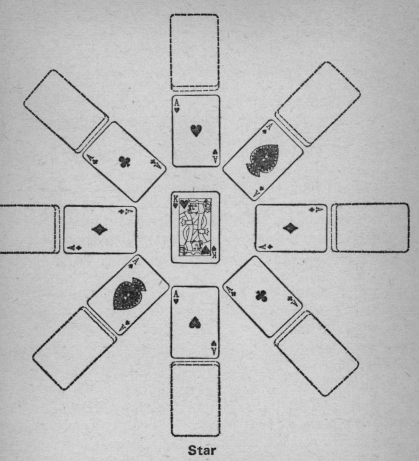

Star

sequence of suit on foundation aces, which are laid aside as exposed to form a foundation row.

The bottom card for the time being of each depot column, the dealing card and the top card for the time being of the discard pile are exposed and playable to foundations in ascending sequence of suit and to depots in descending sequence of alternate colour. Sequences and parts of sequences must not be moved in block.

When all available cards have been played from the original layout, deal through the pack one card at a time to foundations and depots wherever possible, otherwise face upwards to a discard pile.

When all the cards of a depot column have been played the resulting space may be filled by any exposed card. Only one deal through the pack is allowed.

97. Thirteen

Deal across a foundation row of thirteen cards in sequence of alternate colour from a seven to a six. Then deal twenty-two reserve packets of four cards each and one of three cards. The top card for the time being of each reserve packet is exposed and playable to foundations in ascending sequence of colour except for the foundation on the extreme right which is built up in ascending sequence of alternate colour. When all the cards of a reserve pile have been played the resulting space is *not* filled.

One redeal is allowed. Lift the reserve, shuffle and lay out again in packets of four, any extra cards forming a packet of their own.

98. Triple Line

Deal three rows of twelve cards face upwards, each row overlapping the one above, to form twelve depot columns. Exposed aces and aces exposed in play are laid aside as foundations.

The object of the game is to build the whole pack in ascending sequence of suit on foundations.

The bottom card for the time being of each depot column, the dealing card and the top card for the time being of the discard pile are exposed and playable singly in ascending sequence of suit to foundations and in descending sequence of suit to depots. No sequence or part of a sequence may be moved in block from one depot to another.

When the cards of a depot column have all been played, the resulting space may be filled by any exposed card.

When all available cards in the original layout have been played, deal from the pack one card at a time to foundations and depots or, if a card will not fit, to a discard pile, the top card of which is always playable. No redeal is allowed.

99. West End

This is a complicated and difficult patience often played on the pavements of Leicester Square by impatient shoe-cleaners.

Deal from left to right a row of eleven cards face upwards. Take out any suitable aces and kings to begin a foundation row, filling their places by dealing from the pack, and send others to join them as they are exposed in play, the foundation row to consist eventually of one king and one ace from each suit.

The object of the game is to build the pack in ascending sequence of suit on foundation aces and descending sequence of suit on foundation kings.

When you have played all suitable cards to foundations from the original row, deal a second row of eleven cards beneath the first. The three cards at the left of this row and all the cards of the original row are exposed and playable to foundations if they will fit, their places being filled from the pack. Continue dealing rows of eleven cards until the pack is exhausted. After each row has been dealt suitable exposed cards may be played to foundations and their places filled from the pack. Only the bottom card for the time being of each of the three left-hand columns are at this stage considered to be exposed and playable.

When the pack has been dealt through, the bottom card for the time being of every column is considered to be exposed and may be played to foundations as described, and to depots in upward and downward sequence, upward changing to downward and vice versa at will. A sequence or part of a sequence ending in an exposed card may be moved in block from depot to depot if it will fit.

When all the cards of a column have been played, the resulting space may be filled by an exposed card or a sequence ending in an exposed card. A card or cards may at any time be moved from one foundation to another if they will fit.

When the patience is blocked one grace is allowed – a single card may be moved from the bottom to the top of a depot column.

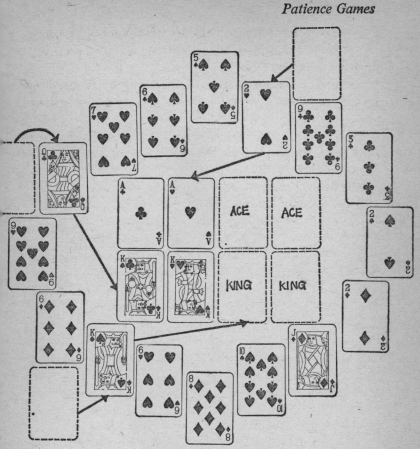

Wheel of Fortune

100. Wheel of Fortune

The two packs are kept separate. From the first pack deal a circle of sixteen depot cards; in the centre of the circle lay an ace and a king of each suit as they appear in play.

121

The object of the game is to build both packs down from kings, up from aces, in sequence of suit.

Play from the original sixteen to foundations, fill the spaces, then deal round again, covering the first depots, play again, deal and play and deal and play and et cetera and so forth and so on.

When an ascending and a descending sequence meet like two men on moving staircases cards can be transferred from one foundation to another. When the pack has been dealt through, the top card of a depot pile may be used to fill any vacancy in 'the wheel'.

Fun on Wheels

by Mary Danby

Ever been bored on a car journey? Never again, with this feast of fun from Armada Books!

Pages of . . . talking games, action games, 'through-the-window' games – quizzes and puzzles – stories – songs – things to make – and a whole carload of jokes, riddles and cartoons.

Happy travelling!

Armada

Make Your Own Presents

HAL DANBY

The best presents are those you make yourself – and
they're the most fun to give.

Here's an exciting book which launches Armada's new
Hobbies and Leisure list. It's full of super ideas for
presents to give all your family and friends. Most of them
can be made easily and cheaply – often from odds and
ends you can find around the house.

The step-by-step instructions are fully illustrated – and
there are presents to make for everyone:

How about a hanging plant basket for Mum, a table lamp
for Dad, or a topsy-turvey doll for a younger sister?
You could make a woolly car stopper for the
garage in an afternoon. Or what about a set of photograph
drink coasters for Grandma?

(Or you could give the book as a present and hope
someone makes one of these presents for you!)

Armada

The Armada Quiz & Puzzle Books
Nos. 1-5

Boost your brain power and have hours of puzzling fun solving the hundreds of different quizzes in this popular Armada series.

Pick your favourite puzzle – names, pictures, anagrams, codes, magic squares, pets, mysteries, sport, history, spelling, doodles, and many, many more. Sharpen your wits and get puzzling!

Have you discovered Armada's latest quiz books? Facts and fun for everyone in six exciting titles:

The Armada Horse & Pony Quiz Books Nos. 1 & 2
by Charlotte Popescu

The Armada Football Quiz Books Nos. 1 & 2
by Gordon Jeffrey

The Armada Animal Quiz Book
by Deborah Holder

Car Quiz
by Hal Danby

Armada

The Armada Book of Jokes and Riddles

compiled by Jonathan Clements

with drawings by Roger Smith

Holidaymaker: Does the water *always* come through the roof like this?
Landlady: Oh no, sir. Only when it rains.

Announcing . . . the first torture-chamber to appear in paperback!

Do you want to drive your friends around the bend?
See your enemies go green and shrivel up?
Giggle yourself silly?
You do?
Then come on in – and laugh till your ears drop off!

And make sure you don't miss the craziest collection of fun and frivolity ever to be trapped between book covers – Jonathan Clements' latest mixture of mirth and madness.

Crazy — But True!

with more drawings by Roger Smith

A feast of fascinating facts to flummox your family and flabbergast your friends. For instance . . .

Gorillas can't swim.
The average man shaves 30 feet of whiskers off his face during his lifetime.
The Ancient Greeks invented the haggis.
 – and hundreds more gems of useless information!
PLUS: The Amazing Perpetual Calendar – The Electrifying Magic Age Table – and a Fantastically Fiendish Quiz!

Armada

The Armada Book of Fun
and
The Second Armada Book of Fun
compiled by Mary Danby

Butler: The invisible man's outside
Lord Prune: Tell him I can't see him

I sat next to the Duchess at tea;
It was just as I feared it would be;
   Her rumblings abdominal
   Were simply phenomenal,
And everyone thought it was me!

Two hilarious helpings of ridiculous riddles, riotous
rhymes, crazy cartoons and preposterous puns, let alone
loony limericks and jokes by the score!

And you'll find all your favourite cartoon characters in:
The Armada Books of Cartoons
and
The Second Armada Book of Cartoons

Laughs Unlimited!

Armada

Armada books are chosen by children all over the world. They're designed to fit your pocket, and your pocket money too – why not build up your own Armada library? There are hundreds of exciting titles and favourite series to collect, and their bright spines look marvellous on any bookshelf. Armada have something for everyone:

Books by popular authors like **Enid Blyton – Malcolm Saville – Elinor Brent-Dyer – Alfred Hitchcock**, etc.

The best mysteries and most exciting adventure stories.

Favourite characters like **Jennings – William – Nancy Drew – The Hardy Boys – Biggles – The Three Investigators – The Lone Piners – and many, many more.**

Pony Books by the Pullein-Thompson sisters, Mary Gervaise and Judith Berrisford.

A wonderful collection of famous children's stories.

Ghost books to make your hair stand on end!

A terrific collection of **quiz, puzzle and fun books** to entertain you for hours.

These are just a few of the good things Armada has in store for you.

If you'd like a complete up-to-date list of Armada books, send a stamped, addressed envelope to:
Armada Books,
14 St James's Place,
London SW1